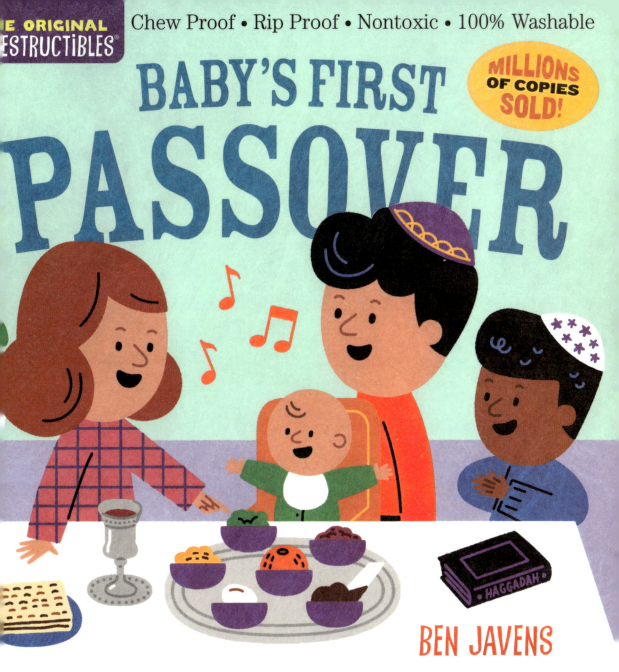

Passover is here!

Our table is set with the seder plate.

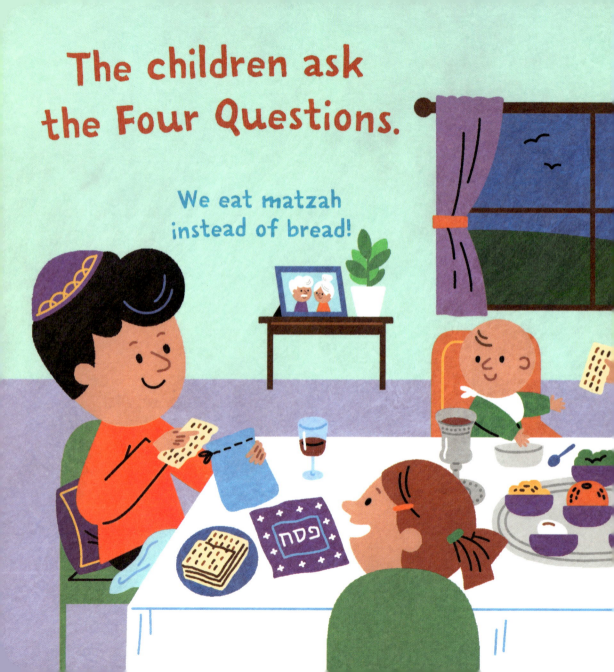

How is this night different from all other nights?

Let's open the door for Elijah.

THE ORIGINAL INDESTRUCTIBLES®

For ages 0 and u[p]

BOOKS BABIES CAN REALLY SINK THEIR GUMS INTO!

It's Passover! What do we eat? *Matzah!*
What do we sing? *"Dayenu"!*
What do we say? *Chag sameach!*

Celebrate the night different from all others in a book that's INDESTRUCTIBL[E]

Dear Parents: INDESTRUCTIBLES are built for the way babies "read": with their hands and mouths. INDESTRUCTIBLES won't rip or tear and are 100% washable. They're made for baby to hold, grab, chew, pull, and bend.

CHEW ALL THESE AND MOR[E]

$5.99 US / $8.99 Can.
ISBN 978-1-5235-1774-9

9 781523 517749   50599

Copyright © 2022 by Indestructibles, LLC. Used under license.
Illustrations copyright © 2022 by Workman Publishing Co., Inc.
All rights reserved.
Library of Congress Cataloging-in-Publication Data is available.
WORKMAN is a registered trademark of Workman Publishing Co., Inc.
First printing November 2022 | 10 9 8 7 6 5 4 3 2 1

All INDESTRUCTIBLES books have been safety-tested and me[et or]
exceed ASTM-F963 and CPSIA guideli[nes.]
INDESTRUCTIBLES is a registered trademark of Indestructibles, L[LC.]
Contact specialmarkets@workman.com regard[ing]
special discounts for bulk purcha[ses.]
Printed in Ch[ina]

WORKMAN PUBLISHING CO., INC. 225 Varick Street, New York, NY 10014 • indestructiblesinc.com